THE BEGINNING

OF JUDGMENT

PRINCIPLES & PROCEDURES FOR

BIBLICAL CHURCH DISCIPLINE

STEVE PIXLER

THE BEGINNING

OF JUDGMENT

PRINCIPLES & PROCEDURES FOR

BIBLICAL CHURCH DISCIPLINE

STEVE PIXLER

Published by
Continuum Ministry Resources

5200 David Strickland Road Fort Worth, TX 76119
©2006, 2013 Steve Pixler

Published in the United States by
Continuum Ministry Resources
5200 David Strickland Rd.
Fort Worth, TX 76119

Unless otherwise identified, all scripture quotations are taken from King James Version.

Printed in the United States of America
Cover design by Zeit Designs

ISBN-13: 978-0-9796261-6-6
ISBN-10: 0-9796261-6-1

Library of Congress Control Number: 2013933315

TABLE OF CONTENTS

Introduction

"For the time is come that judgment must begin at the house of God: and if it first begin at us, what shall the end be of them that obey not the gospel of God?" (I Peter 4:17)

Judgment Must Begin at the House of God

Peter's statement concerning the beginning of judgment has long been the subject of much discussion. We have often considered the beginning of judgment primarily as a question of timing, as a question of when a man's accountability before God begins. This has been considered with particular regard to the issue of divorce and remarriage. But Peter's statement concerns much more than the demarcation of the church's jurisdiction in time. Peter is not concerned so much with when judgment begins as he is where it begins.

God's judgment begins with His own house, which is the church. God shall judge the earth and all that dwell therein, but He shall start with His own people. It has always been so. The Old Testament is filled with examples where God promised that His judgment would begin with His people and then overtake the surrounding nations. The New Testament continues the theme of unique responsibility for those who have been called by His name.

God is expecting more from those He has saved and filled with His Spirit than those who stumble through life without His gracious direction. Jesus said, "For unto whomsoever much is given, of him shall be much required" (Luke 12:48). Judgment is coming upon this world, but the church shall be purged in judgment first. "Whose fan is in his hand, and he will thoroughly purge his floor, and gather his wheat into the garner; but he will burn up the chaff with unquenchable fire" (Matthew 3:12). The Lord shall judge His people first of all.

Peter also speaks about the shame of Christians who suffer punishment before the bench of secular law because they do not keep the law of God. Peter insists that the only time a Christian should be haled before a secular magistrate is when they are prosecuted for being a Christian. Then, they should feel honored to suffer persecution valiantly for the name of Christ.

This is the thrust of Peter's remarks. He is determined to remind Christians that they are called to uphold a higher standard of conduct than the unbelievers around them. Christians uphold the law of God, and God's judgment shall begin with them, to reward and punish them according to their works.

The Reproach of Injustice

The church should be a place of judgment and justice, representing God's perfect law in the earth. There is no greater reproach than when the world observes that the church is a place of lawlessness and injustice. Much of the world's cynicism toward Christians is a result of the deplorable behavior of Christians. The church was destined by God to be a holy place where the law of God is fulfilled and the remarkable justice of that law manifested to the world. We cannot hope to convince the world of the superiority of our way of life and the truth of our doctrine if we cannot ensure justice among our members. If we allow injustice to run rampant in the Christian community by refusing to settle disputes, confront egregious sins and enforce doctrinal purity, then how can we convince the world community that the Word of God is the only viable rule of life? If *we* do not believe in the Word of God enough to obey it, then why should *they*?

The Cross we preach is the centerpiece of all cosmic and divine justice. It is the true beginning of all judgment. At the Cross, God's infinite judgment and mercy were displayed. Our lack of judgment within the church betrays the cause for which Christ died and we were saved: to reveal to the world the power and wisdom of the Cross. Our failure to reckon right judgment makes a mockery of the Cross, where the holiness of God was so pure that it demanded that the penalty of sin be paid, and the love of God so strong that it demanded that Christ be the One who paid it. Our insistence on godly judgment is an insistence on lifting up the Cross where judgment begins. The church is where the Cross is preached. Thus, judgment must begin at the house of God.

The Old Testament is replete with passages where the Lord God inveighed against the injustice that defiled the land of Israel and covered the violence in her streets. God grew intensely angry with those who perverted judgment and tolerated oppression. But we, too, are guilty of perverting judgment. We do so in two ways: (1) by refusing to judge the sins in our midst; and (2) by judging sins arbitrarily outside of the procedures established by Christ in the New Testament.

The perversion of judgment promotes injustice, which is lawlessness and iniquity. The rule of law is the basis for all societal stability. Contempt for law and order brings anarchy and civil unrest. Injustice and arbitrary judgments create confusion and chaos. But God's law and order bring peace. We all have witnessed the confusion created by Christians who failed to adjudicate matters properly according to the protocol of Scripture. We have also witnessed the peace of God prevail when men and women were careful to pursue right judgment in the right way. We must "follow peace with all men" by making certain that our congregations pursue biblical justice through biblical church discipline.

One aspect of ecclesiology that must be emphasized is the judicial nature of the local church. The Lord Jesus set up the church to function as an ecclesiastical court with supreme jurisdiction and sovereignty over the conduct and behavior of its members. Jesus declared that whatever we bind on earth will have been bound already in heaven. When we judge a matter according to the Word of God, we are realizing on earth the will of God in the heavens. We cannot hope to reflect the will of heaven if we handle matters in an off-hand or thoughtless way. Jesus declared that "my judgment is just; because I seek not mine own will" (John 5:30). We cannot hope to obtain justice if we prosecute matters according to our own arbitrary idea of what is best. We must diligently seek the will of God in every case.

ANTICIPATING THE LAST JUDGMENT

We shall see in a moment that Christians can submit to the judgment of God now and prevent their condemnation at the last day. We can do so by rendering biblical judgment against sin among our members. We can anticipate the Judgment through the judicial process of New Testament church discipline. We still have time to repent as long as we are here on earth. But if we delay the confrontation of our sin until the final judgment, there shall be no opportunity for repentance and reconciliation. As the preacher so wisely said, "in the place where the tree falleth, there it shall be" (Ecclesiastes 11:3).

We may choose to anticipate the Judgment while mercy is still available, or we may delay dealing with sin until it is too late. "Some men's sins are open beforehand, going before to judgment; and some men they follow after" (1 Timothy 5:24). But either way, we shall "all appear before the judgment seat of Christ; that every one may receive the things done in his body, according to that he hath done, whether it be good or bad" (2 Corinthians 5:10).

The purpose of this book is to emphasize the need for biblical judgment and church discipline among our congregations. We must not continue to tolerate the unbridled sin of lawless men or the perverted judgment of leaders who prosecute the disobedient at their injudicious whim and pleasure. We must insist that God's judgment, meted out at the Cross and extended into our congregations by His continued presence, is the only equitable and fair judgment. God alone is just. Thus, we can offer justice only as we enact and reflect the justice of God.

God's justice is revealed in the Cross, where forgiveness is offered to all who will repent. God forgives, and therefore, we are compelled to forgive. But God's forgiveness demands repentance, and our forgiveness must demand repentance as well. We cannot expect the blessings of God upon obedience if we are not willing to accept the curse of God upon disobedience. We are called to initiate judgment. And judgment begins at the house of God.

APOSTOLICS AND CHURCH DISCIPLINE

The subject of church discipline is one that has been sorely neglected among Apostolics, at least in its purely biblical form. Some churches ignore altogether matters requiring discipline, while others deal with them in a very peremptory and arbitrary fashion. But such random treatments are counterproductive to the health of the church. The New Testament offers specific instructions for the adjudication of disputes between brothers and sisters, disobedience to standards of godly conduct and doctrinal deviation. The judicial procedures for prosecution, conviction and restoration are outlined clearly for us to follow.

We must recognize the paramount importance of proper biblical procedure, study the procedures diligently and follow them closely. God's way is always the best way. We must insist on following His express instructions in every case.

We shall consider briefly several passages to discover the proper procedures and guidelines established by the New Testament for church discipline. We shall consider three areas of judicial action: (1) disputes between members; (2) disobedience to godly standards of conduct; and (3) deviation from biblical doctrine. This paper is of necessity a simplified treatment of a vast and involved subject that holds wide-ranging implications for Christian practice and polity. But possibly a brief glance at biblical church discipline shall provoke a much closer look at the subject overall and encourage a stricter adherence to New Testament procedures.

CHAPTER ONE

DISPUTES BETWEEN MEMBERS

THE SERMON ON THE MOUNT

Matthew 5:21-26. The first passage we shall consider is the portion of Jesus' Sermon on the Mount where He raises the issue of disputes between brethren. Here, Jesus strengthens the requirements of righteousness under the New Covenant. The Old Covenant had stipulated that men shall stand in danger of the judgment if they are guilty of murder. But, under the New Covenant, the claims of righteousness go even further. Christ reproves the man who becomes angry with his brother without cause and assaults his brother with harsh words and vicious name-calling. Jesus shows the precipitous decline of personal attack as it deteriorates from being angry with your brother beyond all reason, to accusing a man of being a silly, mindless fellow,[1] to finally condemning him of total depravity and spiritual worthlessness.[2] Jesus equates this kind of *ad hominem* attack with murder.

ANGRY WITHOUT CAUSE

The amazing thing about the dreadful process Jesus describes is that it begins with being angry "without cause."[3] This does not mean that there is no reason at all for the dispute, but that the seriousness of the infraction does not match the level of rancor it has occasioned. Indeed, the entire imbroglio is unnecessary. Most disputes are based on a simple misunderstanding that could have been settled quickly with just a few moments of humble inquiry. Jesus' teaching should cause us to develop the ingrained habit of refusing to grow angry with a brother on unsubstantiated charges. We must make certain that we are not angry without cause. Unjustified anger leads to groundless charges and lying insults. Unjustified anger

---

[1] This is the meaning of "raca" in verse 22.

[2] This is the meaning of "fool" in verse 22.

[3] Some manuscripts omit "without cause."

quickly deteriorates into a surreal hatred that demonizes its adversaries and makes reconciliation near impossible.

Most people are not as evil as their opponents believe. But by permitting their anger to grow on the imagination that feeds it, men reckon their enemies to be totally worthless people and incapable of restoration. This is usually nonsense. Most disputes arise between generally decent men and women who become sworn enemies in mindless wars, drawing entrenched battle lines around exaggerated issues that could have been settled in just a few moments of charitable conversation. Again, Jesus equates this unreasonable hatred with *murder*. Then, Jesus gives us specific guidelines that we may prevent these misunderstandings and promote unity among brethren.

APPROACHING THE ALTAR

And yet, as we have noted above, the first man is angry "without cause," which means he is angry out of all proportion to the sin committed against him. Neither man is justified before God in their present condition. The first man is angry and has become a spiritual murderer, and the second man is complicit in the first man's rage as long as he does nothing to rectify his error and resolve the conflict. The defendant should feel the urgency to reconcile with his brother so that he may correct what he has done wrong. He should also feel the responsibility to deliver his accuser from the snare he has cast for his feet by sinning against him. Though the plaintiff is solely responsible for his overreaction, Jesus portrays the defendant as partially responsible for the plaintiff's initial anger.

This is a fundamental principle of Christ's teaching on church discipline. We are taught to pursue reconciliation and restoration for the salvation of our brother and not for our own personal benefit. All disciplinary procedures must operate according to the selfless principle of the Cross: "Look not every man on his own things, but every man also on the things of others" (Philippians 2:4).

In this passage, the guilty party bears the onus for reconciliation. In Matthew 18 (as we shall see below), Jesus places the responsibility for reconciliation on the man who was wronged. But here, making things right is the task of the defendant. Ideally, both the plaintiff and the defendant should feel the responsibility to initiate reconciliation. As one man said, they should meet in the street on the way to each other's house!

LEAVE YOUR GIFT AT THE ALTAR

At this point in Jesus' narrative, the plaintiff is angered to the point of hatred, and the defendant is blithely proceeding to his turn at the altar. But when the second man approaches the altar, something wonderful happens. The second man remembers that he has offended a brother who now wrongly considers him a mindless and worthless fellow. In a moment of tender worship, the offender feels the tug of the Spirit compelling him to go and make things right with his brother.

Jesus instructs the worshipper to leave his gift at the altar, step quietly out of line, and go in search of his brother, who is presumably somewhere in the Temple complex preparing to offer sacrifices for him and his family. The offender approaches the offended and succeeds in effecting a genuine reconciliation. He may then return to the altar and offer his gifts. The example Jesus offers is a beautiful model of forgiveness and restoration and introduces several themes that compel closer scrutiny.

THE SPIRITUAL EFFECT OF BROTHERLY RELATIONSHIPS

First, Jesus' teaching indicates that our relationship with God is directly affected by our relationship with our brother. Here, in a moment of tender devotion, the Spirit of the Lord recalls to our mind actions and attitudes that have become a stumbling block to our brother, and the gentle conviction of the Spirit compels us to approach in meekness and humility the one we have wronged. We are instructed to leave our gift at the altar and return to worship after reconciliation has been accomplished.

This suggests that God will not accept our offering until we have made things right with our brother. This has profound implications for all forms of Christian devotion including prayer and worship. God does not accept our prayers as long as we have unresolved issues with others. The Apostle John insists in his epistles that our love for God is demonstrated by our love for the brethren and that God refuses to accept the love of a man who despises another. We cannot be right with God if we are not right with our brother.

THE INITIATIVE FOR RECONCILIATION

Second, Jesus insists, as we noted above, that the initiative for reconciliation in this case lies with the offender. If we know that our brother holds a bitter grudge against us that causes him to stand in danger of eternal judgment, we are responsible to approach him and humbly seek his forgiveness. We live under the imperative of making things right with the one we have offended for the benefit of our relationship with God and for the salvation of the one we have caused to stumble.

EAGER FOR RECONCILIATION

Third, we must approach the offended party eager to effect reconciliation. "Agree with thine adversary quickly, whiles thou art in the way with him" (v. 25). Too often, we approach those we have wronged with self-justifying explanations calculated to mitigate our guilt. But Jesus requires that we accept the blame quickly and make peace with all due haste. This does not mean that we hurry past an honest confrontation of our actions or make light of the grievance, but rather that we accept quickly complete responsibility for our actions. We should not be reluctant to either admit that we are wrong or express our deep regret for the hurt we have caused. This is the proper Christian attitude.

This simple procedure of self-discipline alone would prevent the spread of division and malice within the Christian community. If we would cultivate a humble sensitivity that allows the Spirit to convict us of our need to seek reconciliation with our brother, then conflicts would be resolved on a personal level without ever requiring the public rebuke and censure of official church discipline. If handled properly, such disputes would never make it to "the judge and the officer" to whom Christ referred, which, in our case, would be the presbytery of the local church (vs. 25, 26).

We must cultivate tenderness toward God in worship so that He may convict and remind us of wrongs we have done against our brother. We must recognize that our relationship with God is contingent upon our willingness to cultivate brotherly love and settle disputes with humility and honesty. And should a dispute arise, we must sense the urgency of the Spirit that compels us to leave our gift at the altar and settle the dispute quickly before it has a chance to develop into a bitter feud. We also must acknowledge that our actions could cause someone else to be called into judgment for their anger and bitterness toward us. We must be willing to settle the dispute, not only for our own salvation, but also for the salvation of our brother. And we must be willing to admit our guilt quickly and do whatever it takes to make the matter right. Our meek attitude will promote a smooth reconciliation. "A soft answer turneth away wrath" (Proverbs 15:1). If we diligently follow this procedure, then the further prosecution of the case will be unnecessary.

JUDICIAL PROCEDURES

Matthew 18:15-20. In our second passage, the Lord approaches from another angle the subject of settling disputes between brethren. In Matthew 5, the offended party has responded with anger and accusation, and the burden of reconciliation rests upon the offender. But in Matthew 18, Christ places the burden of reconciliation upon the offended party. These two passages, if taken together, leave no excuse for not settling disputes peacefully and privately. As we noted above, both the offender and the offended have an obligation to pursue reconciliation. There is no excuse for unsettled disputes between Christians.

Also in Matthew 18, the Lord outlines very specific judicial procedures for individuals and officials in the church to follow.

The Lord instructs the offended man to pursue a three-step process, of which, the first two are to be conducted in private:

PRIVATE ENTREATY

(1) Approach your brother privately. If he responds to your entreaty, then you have gained you brother without undue publicity. (2) If he will not listen to you privately, then approach him accompanied by two or three witnesses to verify your case and to assist you as you attempt reconciliation. If he will listen to you and those accompanying you, then, again, you have gained your brother with minimal exposure.

PUBLIC CONFRONTATION

However, if he will not listen to you and your witnesses, then the process is ratcheted up to a new and very unpleasant level. (3) The offended party must then file formal charges against the offender and bring the matter before the government of the local church, at which point, the process becomes official judicial proceedings. If the offender will hear the church, again, we have won our brother. If he will not hear the church, then the church is required to judge the matter and excommunicate the unrepentant brother. Jesus declares that he is to be treated "as a heathen man and a publican" (v.17). This is not done arbitrarily to satisfy the whim of the powerful or the vengeful, but it must be done to save the soul of the unrepentant.

The offended party *must* press the charges. He is not allowed to simply drop the matter, for it is his brother's salvation at stake, not his. The offended party, if he keeps the right spirit, may be wronged and be saved. But the offender cannot remain wrong and be saved. His sin will meet him at the judgment. Again, this is the fundamental motive for church discipline. We are pressing charges to gain our brother, not to destroy him. All church discipline is remedial. Thus, the disciplinary process is more for our brother's salvation than for our satisfaction.

THE VERDICT OF EARTH AND HEAVEN

This is where the church must accept its judicial role and responsibility. The church must perform as an ecclesiastical court and press the charges to a final verdict. Jesus assures us that the decision of the church is recognized—indeed, it is *anticipated*—by heaven. Jesus promised, "Whatsoever ye shall bind on earth shall be bound in heaven: and whatsoever ye shall loose on earth shall be loosed in heaven" (v. 18). The tense of Jesus' words in the original actually indicates that whatever we bind and loose on earth "shall have been" bound and loosed in heaven. This means that the verdict of the church, when the charges are prosecuted and decided according to Scripture, reflects the verdict of heaven.

It is important to emphasize this reality. Jesus declared that He is personally present when such decisions are made (v. 20). A local church that judges a case fairly and biblically is deciding the case with the divine endorsement of the Lord Jesus Christ. If the offender refuses to repent and decides to worship elsewhere, his worship will not be received by heaven. He is considered by the church and by the Lord "as a heathen man and a publican" (v. 17). The judgment passed is binding and recognized by heaven regardless of anyone's refusal to acknowledge it.

Furthermore, the sentence of dismissal and excommunication from the Body of Christ can only be remedied by the church that enacted the judgment. Another congregation may choose to ignore the judgment of the church. But if the matter was properly and biblically adjudicated, then heaven honors the decision. An individual judged *biblically* can never escape his judgment without repentance. We must make it right to be right.

Chapter Two

Disobedience to Godly Standards of Conduct

Introductory Principles in Paul's Teaching

1 Corinthians 5:1-6:8. We must note several things very briefly in our third passage. First, the sin of the man discussed in 1 Corinthians 5 was a notorious public sin (5:1, 2; *cf.* 2 Corinthians 2:6). Therefore, he forfeited the private approach of Matthew 18. Matthew 18 deals primarily with disputes between brethren, but the principles outlined there would apply also in cases of sin that had not yet become public. We should give disobedient Christians, even those involved in gross immorality, the opportunity to find repentance and restoration privately. But, as noted, this individual forfeited this consideration when he flaunted his sin before the view of the entire church. Thus, Paul passes over steps one and two of Matthew 18 and moves directly to the public confrontation of this man's sin. A public sin demands public rebuke.

Second, the judicial authority of the church is simply assumed and asserted. Paul wastes no time defending the right of the church to judge its members and excommunicate them. His only reference to the judicial prerogative of the church is astonishment that they have not enacted it (5:1, 2).

Third, Paul asserts that an unwillingness to deal with sin in the congregation is a result of arrogance. This point is generally missed. Paul does not share the opinion of some that authority equals arrogance. He says exactly the opposite. A refusal to exercise proper authority is rooted in arrogance. The apostle was stunned that the church was not heartbroken by the sin parading before them every service. Indeed, they were rather nonchalant about it. Corinth should have been mourning like the prophets of old who wept day and night for the sins of their people.

Wherever genuine humility and the fear of the Lord abide, rampant sin and disobedience will be confronted. Unchecked sin is a result of unchecked pride.

Further, Paul indicates that issues requiring discipline must be judged by the appropriate congregational authorities. In Matthew 5, Jesus spoke of the judge and the officer. In Matthew 18, He spoke of the church hearing the matter. Here, Paul speaks of his unique authority to judge the situation as the apostle of the church. Later, he sarcastically refers to the inability of the Corinthian congregation to judge the smallest matters by calling on them to impanel judges from the least esteemed in the church (6:4). He decries this sad state of affairs and rebukes them for not having appointed wise men to represent the church and judge legal disputes between brethren (6:5). The Corinthian church was not accustomed to functioning as an ecclesiastical court, and thus, they failed to fulfill the mandate given by Jesus to address the egregious sin openly flaunted and tolerated in their midst. They failed to learn the procedures for church discipline, and they failed to understand the profound importance of bringing such cases to judgment.

Paul insists that the authority of the church is endorsed and enforced by the authority of Jesus Christ

(5:4, 5). This clearly mirrors the declaration of Jesus in Matthew 18 that the judgment of the church reflects the judgment of heaven. Paul also reiterates the teaching of Christ when he indicates that the purpose of church discipline is for the salvation of both the individual and the church body (5:5; 6:15-20; *cf.* 2 Corinthians 2:1-11). Excommunication is remedial if it produces genuine repentance and restoration.

COMMUNION AND DISCIPLINE

In verses 6-8, we encounter an interesting development in the subject of church discipline as Paul introduces the Passover/Communion motif. "Your glorying is not good. Know ye not that a little leaven leaveneth the whole lump? Purge out therefore the old leaven, that ye may be a new lump, as ye are unleavened. For even Christ our Passover is sacrificed for us: Therefore let us keep the feast, not with old leaven, neither with the leaven of malice and wickedness; but with the unleavened bread of sincerity and truth."

Paul insists that allowing the sinner to remain in fellowship with the body corrupts the communion of the body, which is the communion of the saints with Christ and with one another. But there is an implicit connection in Paul's thought with the removal of the unrepentant brother from the fellowship of believers and excommunication from the Table of the Lord's Supper. In verse 11, Paul forbids the church "to eat" with the recalcitrant man. But this eating together is much more than the casual eating of a potluck dinner. Rather, the meal of which Paul speaks is the feast of the new covenant Passover, the Lord's Supper.

Thus, the Table of the Lord's Supper emerges into our view as the judgment bar from which the church executes and enforces its judicial decisions. The unrepentant brother is cut off from the body by being formally and publicly banned from the Table. This is reminiscent of Old Testament practice where sinners were cut off from the congregation and banned from feasts and sacrifices. Excommunication from the Lord's Supper is how the church retains sins (*cf.* John 20:23). The Lord's Supper is the communion of the Body of Christ and sinners must be banned from the communion (5:6-13).[4] Guests may visit

---

[4] *Cf.* John 13 where Judas is "cut off" from the mercy of God by being sent away from the Table. *Cf. also* I Corinthians 10:14-22; 11:27-34.

our services and sit on our pews, but they must not be admitted to the Lord's Table unless they are living under the authority and sanction of the church's judgment and are deemed worthy of the Lord's body (2 Corinthians 11:27-34).

The Table of the Lord is a table of judgment, for good or for evil. It brings either blessing or cursing. Of course, we must observe the Lord's Supper much more frequently if we plan to practice the principles of church discipline on a regular basis. A judiciary that holds court once a year has little practical power to stem the tide of lawless behavior. The judgments of the church must be consistent and sure if we hope to have any influence over those within our jurisdiction. We must observe the Lord's Supper often enough that we can render judgments while the details of the case are still within the recall of recent memory.

LAWSUITS BETWEEN CHRISTIANS

Paul continues in his discussion of the church as the arbiter of Christian disputes with a diatribe against the practice of taking fellow Christians to secular courts. There are many points to consider in his discussion and much to be learned. But one of the most important parts of his critique is his point concerning the willingness to suffer wrong (6:7). Paul is outraged that Christian charity is so lacking among Corinthian believers that they are dragging their brothers and sisters into lawsuits over the slightest provocation (6:2).[5] Yet, this vengeful and litigious attitude is outlined against the backdrop of a nonchalant lack of interest in pressing charges over an issue that really matters — the incestuous relationship of a man who has brazenly married his father's wife.[6] The entire episode demonstrates a bizarre lack of judgment.

COVERING SINS WITH LOVE

And yet, the principle of a willingness to suffer wrong comes ringing through loud and clear in Paul's discussion. Indeed, this principle should be the foundational principle of all church discipline. *We should prosecute only the cases that are a matter of being saved or lost.* If an offense can be overlooked and forgotten without endangering anyone's relationship with God, then we should dismiss the transgression as nothing and refuse to be upset about it.

---

[5] Paul describes their disputes as "the smallest matters."

[6] Probably his stepmother.

As stated in another scripture, we must let love cover a multitude of sins. But if the matter is so serious as to place the soul of either the offender or the offended at risk, then we must move ahead with procedures for confrontation and reconciliation. Can the matter be dismissed? Can we allow love to cover the sin and refuse to hold it against our brother? If so, then we should. We must maintain a balanced outlook. Overlook the offenses we can and prosecute the ones we cannot. Let love for our brother and a genuine concern for his salvation be the guiding principle that makes the determination.

FORNICATION

Finally, Paul closes his discussion in chapter 6 with some very pointed comments about the sin of fornication. This part of Paul's discussion has particular relevance to the issue of church discipline, for Paul isolates the sin of fornication in a category of its own. He declares that we must, "Flee fornication. Every sin that a man doeth is without the body; but he that committeth fornication sinneth against his own body" (6:18). Fornication is a sin against both the body of the individual and the Body of Christ.

Paul insists that "he which is joined to a harlot is one body" and "he that is joined to the Lord is one spirit" (6:16, 17). Paul declares that those who commit fornication are joined to a harlot while they are joined to the Lord and to the Body of Christ. Thus, they are joining their sin to the Body of Christ at large. As he said earlier, "a little leaven leaveneth the whole lump" (5:6). The church, particularly the local church where the fornicator worships, is affected profoundly by the unique sin of fornication.

Therefore, we must be decisive and aggressive about confronting this particular sin. We must confront the sinner and ensure repentance and restoration. If that fails, then we must enact the judicial procedures set forth in scripture and root out the sin by rooting out the sinner. If the sin will not go, then the sinner must. We cannot excuse and tolerate sin under the guise of a false Christian charity. "Open rebuke is better than secret love" (Proverbs 27:5). The fear of the Lord and the mandate of God's justice require that we react immediately when we are made aware of the transgression.

Furthermore, it is a mere pretense of love that ignores the eternal consequences of sin and stands idly by as disobedient souls plunge headlong into hell. Remember, church discipline is remedial. Our judicial objective is to confront the sinner with his sin and humbly persuade him to repent. A reluctance to confront sin hurts the sinner worse than anyone, though the church itself will pay a dear price for its tolerance.

Some have enacted a "three strikes" policy to rectify the ongoing problem with fornication. This policy follows the procedures of Matthew 18 in confronting the sin privately at the first offense. The second offense is confronted at the second level of prosecution regardless of the lapse of time involved between the first and second offense, and witnesses are called in to participate in the proceedings. The third offense is treated as an obvious absence of true repentance and an expression of habituated sin. Thus, the fornicator is charged automatically and formally before the church and given a final opportunity for repentance. One more violation—the fourth instance—results in immediate expulsion and public excommunication. (Some churches have elected to expel recalcitrant members immediately at the third offense, not giving a final opportunity for repentance and restoration at the public confrontation.)

This policy demands that the final and public exposure of the sin impose punishment without remedy. Pastors who have enacted this policy will not allow someone who has undergone this process to return ever to their local assembly. Some churches elect to release the offenders to attend church elsewhere but forbid them to return ever to the prosecuting assembly. This may seem harsh, but it is a one-of-a-kind response to a one-of-a-kind sin. However a local church decides to address the issue, it must decide to address it. We cannot permit sin to go unchallenged, particularly the sin of fornication.

DISCERNING THE LORD'S BODY

A lack of church discipline arises from a failure to discern the Lord's body. As a result, we persist unworthily in communion with the body and blood of the Lord so beautifully symbolized in the Lord's Supper. But when we catch a glimpse of the holiness of the Body of Christ and the terrible price He paid for our righteousness, then we are brokenhearted at the transgressions of those who trample His blood under foot and continue in sin willfully, doing "despite unto the spirit of grace" (Hebrews 10:29). Therefore, we must be diligent to follow the procedures set forth in scripture to ensure that "the spirit may be saved in the day of the Lord Jesus"—both the spirit of the man and the spirit of the church.

CHAPTER THREE

DEVIATION FROM CHRISTIAN DOCTRINE

FALSE TEACHING WITHIN THE CHURCH

We must note that it is not within the scope of this paper to discuss the proper reaction to those outside the church who seek to draw away disciples from the church through the propagation of false doctrine. Both Paul and John react very strongly to this dire threat, and we must do likewise. But for now, let's focus on the procedures of dealing with those within the church who promote false teaching.

There are several passages in the New Testament that indicate the response of the church toward those within the congregation who promote division with false doctrine. Paul instructs us to "mark them which cause divisions and offences contrary to the doctrine which ye have learned; and avoid them" (Romans 16:7). Paul commanded the Thessalonians to "withdraw yourselves from every brother that walketh disorderly, and not after the tradition which he received of us." And, "if any man obey not our word by this epistle, note that man, and have no company with him, that he may be ashamed" (2 Thessalonians 3:6, 14). He warned Timothy to "turn away" from those who promote error and lead souls astray (2 Timothy 3:5). But these passages give only a brief sketch of our reaction to false doctrine in our midst. They do not give us specific procedures for confronting the error.

CORRECTING DOCTRINAL ERROR

Titus 3:9-11. One passage, however, provides a succinct outline of disciplinary procedure for correcting doctrinal error. Not surprisingly, it aligns rather closely with the procedures we have discussed so far, particularly Matthew 18. Paul charged Titus,

> But avoid foolish questions, and genealogies, and contentions, and strivings about the law; for they are unprofitable and vain. A man that is a heretic after the first and second admonition reject; knowing that he that is such is subverted, and sinneth, being condemned of himself. (Titus 3:9-11)

THE NATURE OF HERETICS

First of all, a heretic is an individual who divides the unanimity of Christian belief. A heretic embraces and promotes doctrines that have not been submitted to careful scrutiny and accepted for dissemination by apostolic consensus. The root of the word transliterated "heretic" literally means, "to choose." A heretic is one who selects his own doctrine without careful comparison and consultation. He refuses, as a matter of principle (if rebellion is a principle!), to accept generally held teachings. The heretic blunders down the overgrown paths of untutored, independent thought and stubbornly stakes his claim deep within the wilderness of ideas where others who made the journey before him refused to dwell.

Generally, a heretic has no desire to submit his opinions for review, for his divisive ideas are merely the fruit of a divisive spirit. Heresy is just another expression of resistance to authority. Thus, a heretic would never countenance the idea of subjecting his views to formal review. The only acceptable public discussion to a heretic is an acrimonious debate. The heretic does not possess the humility to avoid a spectacle. Paul confirms this with his charge that a hardened heretic "is subverted, and sinneth, being condemned of himself" (v. 11). Indeed, the official rejection of a heretic simply confirms and announces the condemnation that he is bringing upon himself with his rebellious and unteachable spirit.

DOCTRINAL CONSENSUS

In the New Testament, the development of doctrine requires a consensus. Nothing is decided independently. The apostolic council in Jerusalem demonstrated this principle in Acts 15 when they convened to decide on the conduct required of Gentile believers. Paul affirms the necessity of consensus in Galatians 1 and 2, where he tells the story of how he compared and confirmed his doctrine with those in Jerusalem who had preached the gospel before him. He makes it clear that his personal revelation was insufficient. He needed the confirmation of his elders and peers. He avers that he would have "run in vain" if he had not been assured that his doctrine harmonized with Peter, James and John (Galatians 2:2). Paul certainly did not express the attitude of a heretic. A heretic could not care less what the elders say. He is convinced he is right against the whole world if necessary. A heretic decides what to believe all by himself.

SINCERE QUESTIONS

On the other hand, a person who is questioning sincerely the teaching of the church will approach those in authority and seek clear answers. Sincere people have tremendous respect for their leaders and are eager to hear their views. They are ready to learn; they just need clarification and explanation. And godly leaders will not resent an honest inquiry. The Apostle Paul wrote the entire Book of 1 Corinthians in response to sincere questions. Questions are not the problem. The problem lies in the attitude of the questioner.

But a heretic will not approach leaders with a proper attitude because he has no respect for their opinion, and that is dangerous ground. The approach of the heretic is to challenge his elders and prove them wrong. Thus, Paul tells Titus to waste no time on a heretic. Give him a couple of fair chances to receive correction and then write him off. Furthermore, Paul also puts all the blame for the condemnation on the heretic. The elders who confront and judge him should bear no sense of guilt or responsibility for his excommunication. He is subverted (bent) and cannot be straightened out (v. 11).

TITUS 3 AND MATTHEW 18

Though it is difficult to say that Paul definitely had Jesus' words in Matthew 18 in mind as he wrote to Titus, we can infer sufficient similarity of purpose to confidently assert that the disciplinary procedures should follow the same pattern. Whether we are dealing with disputes between brethren, disobedience to godly standards of conduct, or deviation from Christian doctrine, we should refuse to prosecute error with summary judgment. Here, as in other instances, we must confront the issue squarely and give the offender a chance to get it right. If the first warning is not sufficient, we should approach our brother again. And here, as in Matthew 18, it would not hurt to establish every word in the mouth of two or three witnesses. If the second admonition fails, then we should reject the heretic. Again, it would only be wise and consistent to follow Matthew 18 again and make this third and final confrontation public so that the church may be warned against continuing in fellowship with a divisive and subversive fellow.

If we are correct in assuming that Paul's teaching in Titus 3 can be harmonized with Christ's teaching in Matthew 18 (and there seems to be no obvious reason we cannot), then we must conclude that all three issues we have discussed[7] follow the same procedures of church discipline.

---

[7] (1) Disputes between members; (2) disobedience to godly standards of conduct; and (3) deviation from biblical doctrine.

CHAPTER FOUR

VARIOUS SCRIPTURES ILLUSTRATING PROCEDURES FOR DISCIPLINE

THE PROPER ATTITUDE OF CHURCH DISCIPLINE

We have noted that Paul rebuked the litigious spirit of the Corinthian church and their inability to discern between significant and insignificant issues. We have distilled from his discussion the principle of never prosecuting a case that can be covered with love and quickly forgotten. We should not confront our brothers and sisters over every minor infraction. But there are times that charges must be pressed forcefully and fully. In those unpleasant instances, we must make certain that we approach the discipline of recalcitrant members with the right spirit. The following passages deal specifically with the attitude of those prosecuting the case when a brother or sister offends. We shall consider them briefly.

A SPIRIT OF MEEKNESS

Galatians 6:1-5. In this passage, Paul teaches us to approach our erring brother with a "spirit of meekness; considering thyself, lest thou also be tempted" (v. 1). We are taught to repudiate the pride inherent in human judgment, recognizing that we are sinners representing the sinless Savior. We are not judging others based on our own perfection, but on the perfect righteousness of Christ and His loving decision to save. Again, discipline is remedial. We are approaching our brother to help him, not to hurt him. The proper approach makes all the difference in the world.

Too often, people confront an erring brother with the attitude of a prosecuting counsel charged with the duty of condemning the guilty to eternal damnation. We must remember that we, too, are sinners forgiven by a loving God, and that our crimes against God, of which we have been freely forgiven, are infinitely greater than any crime that could be committed against us or someone else. We have no inherent right to prosecute anyone. When we confront sin, we are representing Christ and the church. "Bear ye one another's burdens, and so fulfill the law of Christ" (v. 2). Thus, we must maintain the proper attitude of meekness as we accept the task of restoring a brother.

THE NECESSITY OF PRAYER

James 5:13-20. James writes that the afflicted should pray, the merry should sing and the sick should call for the elders of the church to receive prayer. He affirms that "the prayer of faith shall save the sick, and the Lord shall raise him up; and if he have committed sins, they shall be forgiven him" (v. 15). He then states, "Confess your faults one to another, and pray one for another, that ye may be healed. The effectual fervent prayer of a righteous man availeth much" (v. 16) and "Brethren, if any of you do err from the truth, and one convert him; let him know, that he which converteth the sinner from the error of his way shall save a soul from death, and shall hide a multitude of sins" (vs.19-20).

Here we see the confession of sins, prayer for forgiveness and healing and restoration. On occasion, this restoration is effected by the elders who are praying for the sick who may have sinned. And then, there are times when the confession and healing are accomplished among brothers and sisters in the church. Now, certainly Christians must be careful in whom they confide, but the ability to be accountable to a brother and address discreetly issues of weakness and failure can be a great source of healing within the Body of Christ. We should develop the practice of helping one another by the discipline of accountability.

Again, this emphasizes our point that discipline is remedial. We are to pray for one another that we may be healed and "The effectual fervent prayer of a righteous man availeth much" (v. 16). It is noteworthy that this powerful and familiar scripture is set in the context of praying for our brother that he may be healed, both physically and spiritually. Those who secure their brother's restoration are commended by James as one who "converteth the sinner from the error of his way [and] save[s] a soul from death, and [hides] a multitude of sins" (v. 20). What a beautiful description of biblical discipline! We are confronting the sinner to save his soul and cover his sins with a loving rebuke before they are publicly exposed and the sinner is humiliated. Proper discipline seeks to restore the sinner with the least amount of public disgrace to both the individual and the church. Those who eagerly prosecute sinners to humiliate them are themselves in danger of the Judgment. Those who judge shall face the same judgment they have passed on others. We must approach the process of church discipline with the proper attitude of meekness and fear.

James also emphasizes that every attempt at restoration must be preceded by the "effectual fervent prayer of a righteous man" (v. 16). This highlights the *extremely* important principle that fervent prayer must precede any confrontation of sin. We must not confront our brother without praying long and hard over the appropriate manner of approach. We also must make supplication and intercession before the Lord that our brother will respond to our entreaty. We should never approach someone until we have interceded for their salvation with genuine humility. The proper attitude toward the sinner begins in prayer for his restoration. We must not pay them a visit while we are angry and indignant against them for their offense. We must empty ourselves of all emotion except a genuine desire to see the sinner saved. We cannot represent our opinions and feelings. We must represent Christ. As Jesus said, "My judgment is just because I seek not mine own will" (John 5:30). Thus, we must be filled with the mind of Christ in prayer before we proceed. If we are led by the Spirit, then the Lord Jesus will go before us with the gentle conviction of the Holy Ghost, and our earnest entreaty shall confirm what the Spirit has already whispered.

THE POWER OF PRAYER

I John 5:14-17. The Apostle John further confirms the importance of prayer when seeking to restore an errant brother. But John emphasizes more than the necessity of prayer in the process of restoration. He emphasizes the power of prayer, the influence that the intercessor has with God.

Literally, John teaches that the intercessor may ask God for repentance and restoration on the behalf of the sinner and God will grant it. Now, this does not mean that God grants forgiveness for the sinner apart from their repentance and confession. But rather, God guarantees a sort of advance forgiveness based on the atonement of the Cross and the personal intercession of the believer contingent upon the sinner's response. The intercessor may approach the sinner with the assurance that he has the endorsement of heaven. God has promised that He will grant life to the repentant. We do not have to wonder when we press the case against the offender whether or not God shall grant life to them. It is good to know that we have the backing of the Lord Jesus Christ.

The intercessor plays an important role in the process of restoration. The brother who observes another man stumble blindly into a snare of sin "shall ask and He shall give him life for them that sin not unto death" (v. 16). It is somewhat difficult to keep the pronouns straight, but it seems that John is saying that the intercessor shall ask and God shall grant life to the intercessor on the behalf of the sinner. This implies that "life"—the power to restore a man to repentance and healing—is actually given to the intercessor and must be mediated to the sinner by the process of judicial confrontation.

THE RESPONSE TO PRAYER

This confirms our point above that the forgiveness given is contingent upon the sinner's response. Life is granted to the intercessor to be extended to the sinner through the process of confrontation and restoration. Just praying for the sinner is not enough. We must press the charges in those cases where a man's soul is at stake and we are unable to cover his sin with love. In this case, the intercessor becomes an advocate who bears the ability to extend life to the sinner in the form of restoration. If the sinner is unresponsive, then the advocate reluctantly becomes a prosecutor who presses the charges to their final conclusion. In effect, we play a dual role of advocate and prosecutor for sinners, much as God did through Christ at Calvary.

The prayers we pray prior to attempting restoration affect both God and man. We, as the Body of Christ, participate in Christ's intercession before God, and we appeal to the mercy of God on the behalf of sinners. We are assured that God's response will be gracious to those who intercede with Him on the behalf of those who have sinned. Our prayers also affect the sinner. We are assured that our prayers have enlisted the aid of the Holy Spirit in convicting the sinner's heart. Intercessory prayer assures us that God is merciful and ensures that the conviction of the Holy Spirit shall prepare them for our visit. God does not guarantee that the sinner will repent, but He does guarantee us that we shall not approach the sinner empty handed without the assurance of mercy and forgiveness.

This aligns closely with James' emphasis on prayer. We always must pray fervently before we confront an errant brother for three reasons: (1) we should condition our own heart to be emptied of all personal motives and attitudes; (2) we should intercede before the Lord for mercy and the assurance of His gracious involvement in the process; and (3) we should implore the Lord to soften the heart of the sinner that he may be turned from sin to obedience. Church discipline must never be initiated without proper preparation in prayer.

CHAPTER FIVE

CONCLUSION

PROCEDURES OF CHURCH DISCIPLINE

We have outlined the following procedures for church discipline: *First*, we have considered the responsibility of the offender to make things right with the offended. If we have sinned against a brother who is consequently in danger of the judgment for his bitterness against us, then we are responsible to approach our brother in a spirit of humility and eagerness to reconcile quickly. We are instructed by the Lord to leave our gift at the altar, indicating that our worship is not received by the Lord as long as we are at odds with our brother. We must make things right to be right.

Second, we have considered the responsibility of the offended to refuse to become bitter and to confront the offender with their trespass against God and man. There are several fundamental principles that we have outlined that give us definite procedures for this confrontation.

First of all, we must weigh the offense and consider if it is an insignificant infraction that can be overlooked by letting love "cover a multitude of sins." This is determined by asking the question, "Does this offense affect anyone's salvation?" If their relationship with God is at stake, then we must confront them for their benefit, not ours. As we noted: discipline is remedial. It is for their salvation, not for our satisfaction. If it cannot be overlooked, then we must proceed to the next step in the process.

Then, we must spend adequate time in prayer preparing our heart with the proper spirit of meekness, interceding before God for mercy and the assurance of forgiveness for the sinner and imploring God to turn the heart of the sinner and grant him repentance. We must not confront the sinner until we are sure that we have properly vetted our attitude and motives before God. Then, we can approach our brother with a genuine desire to see him restored and saved. Our approach makes all the difference in the world.

Next, we must carefully and humbly confront our brother in hopes of effecting reconciliation and securing his salvation. If our humble entreaty fails, then we must enlist the help of two or three discreet witnesses (possibly the elders of the local church) and confront our erring brother again. The witnesses are included for two reasons: (1) to add their voices to our appeal, hoping that the added persuasion will convince the offender of the urgency for settling the matter; and (2) to be prepared to testify before the church of our efforts to settle the matter in the event that the sinner refuses to reconcile.

If the second attempt at reconciliation fails, then the matter must be brought before the church and properly adjudicated. Until this point, the matter has been handled privately, seeking to avoid public humiliation for both the sinner and the church. The only time we should skip this private process is in the event of a notorious and public sin that has been committed in view of the entire church. We have noted that the church must be prepared to act as an ecclesiastical court. We must allow the case to be judged by wise men in our midst, most likely the presbytery of the local congregation, chaired by the senior pastor. It may not be necessary for the entire congregation to be present for the church to judge the matter if it is allowed that certain reputable men may represent the church and the congregation accepts their judgment as final. However, the matter must be fairly and closely examined, calling into account the offended, the offender and witnesses for both the accused and the accuser. The church must judge the merits of the case against the Word of God. If indeed the offense is proven and upheld, then the church must adjure and compel the offender to repent and be reconciled to his brother.

Finally, if the offender refuses to hear the church, then the church is obligated by Christ to excommunicate the individual. The sinner is denounced publicly and removed from the fellowship of the church. The penalty is enacted and symbolized when the sinner is banned officially from the Table of the Lord's Supper. The church must then consider their wayward brother a "heathen and a publican." We are to have no fellowship with the sinner until he returns to the Lord, the church and his offended brother in repentance and reconciliation.

THE PURPOSE OF CHURCH DISCIPLINE

As we have repeatedly emphasized, the purpose of church discipline is not merely punitive. It is remedial. As the Christian church and representatives of the Kingdom of God, we operate under a strict judicial mandate that must be followed scrupulously. We must render biblical judgment to prevent injustice in our churches. Injustice is a perversion of judgment, which provokes the profound displeasure of God. We are judging souls now to save them from the Judgment to come. Churches that refuse to judge their members now are exposing them to the irremediable judgment at the last day. In the case of proper church discipline, judgment is mercy.

When an individual has been prayerfully and biblically prosecuted, then the judgment of the church reflects accurately the judgment of heaven. The individual is cut off from the Body of Christ regardless of his continued church attendance elsewhere. The wayward brother shall not be recovered until he returns to the judgment seat of the congregation where he was cut off and demonstrates his true repentance and willingness to be reconciled to his brother. Then, the repentant brother is restored immediately to Christian fellowship with God and man.[8] This is the biblical process for the redress of grievances between fellow Christians; flagrant sin in the congregation, particularly the sin of fornication; and deviation from Christian doctrine with its resulting division and heretical schism.

We cannot overemphasize the importance of implementing and following the judicial procedure set forth in the Word of God. Lynch mobs and kangaroo courts are perversions of judgment. The same God who cried against injustice among His people in the Old Testament is crying out against it today. The Judge of all the earth shall do right, and He insists that His people follow His example.[9] God's law restrains the impulse of vigilante justice and promotes due process. No man should be condemned without a hearing. But neither should the lawless be allowed to parade boldly up and down the aisles of our churches without rebuke and censure. We must obtain and maintain the judicial balance

---

[8] *Cf.* 2 Corinthians 2:5-11

[9] *Cf.* Genesis 18:25

that can only come from an honest adherence to the law of God. Judgment must begin at the house of God.